GÉZA SZŐCS
LIBERTY, RATS AND SANDPAPER

Poems translated from the Hungarian
by PAUL SOHAR

ACKNOWLEDGEMENTS

Grateful acknowledgement is due to the editors of the following publications where some of these poems first appeared in earlier versions: *Absinthe, Hunger, Left Curve, Matchbook, Nimrod, Partisan Review, Phoebe, Poets Page, To Topos, Vigil,* and *Big Hammer* (all in the US) and in an anthology *Maradok—I Remain* (Pro-Print, Romania, 1997).

GÉZA SZŐCS
LIBERTY, RATS AND SANDPAPER

Poems translated from the Hungarian
by PAUL SOHAR

Iniquity Press
Irodalmi Jelen Könyvek
2017

Kiadja az Iniquity Press,
Dave Roskos,
illetve a Concord Media Jelen
(Irodalmi Jelen)
Aradon

Published by Iniquity Press,
Dave Roskos
(POB 906 Island Heights,
NJ 08732-0906, USA)
in cooperation with
Concord Media Jelen
(Irodalmi Jelen),
Arad, Romania

Felelős kiadó: Böszörményi Zoltán
Borító: Bege Magdolna

Editor-in Chief: Zoltán Böszörményi
Cover: Magdolna Bege

Honlap: www.irodalmijelen.hu
Nyomda: Ingram Content Group LLC

Website: www.irodalmijelen.hu
Printing House: Ingram Content
Group LLC

ISBN: 978-973-7842-31-2

Table of Contents

Prologue   9

PART I. SELECTED POEMS   11

THE GREAT MARINETTI CAR
(*A nagy Marinetti autó*)   13
LIBERTY, RATS AND SANDPAPER
(*Szabadság...*)   15
THE SHIP PROPELLER
(*A hajócsavar*)   17
A FOUNDLING AMONG EBONY TREES
(*Talált gyerek az ébenfák közt*)   18
THE UNDERGROUND BIRD-WATCHING BLIND
(*A mélyrétegek*)   19
THE BAGPIPER
(*A dudás*)   20
TO THE FOREST LODGE, WHEN?
(*Az erdőházba, mikor?*)   21
THE TWENTY-THIRD SNOWFALL
(*A huszonharmadik hóhullás*)   22
THE REBELS' SUPPER
(*A forradalmárok vacsorája*)   23
(UNFINISHED)
(*befejezetlen*)   24
DRESS UP YOUR INNER TEDDY BEAR
(*Add rá a benned alvó gyanútlan kisgyerekre*)   25
EVENING PRAYER
(*Esti ima*)   26
WINTER SONNET
(*Téli szonett*)   29
LISTENING TO MUHAMMAD ALI
(*Muhammad Ali két verse*)   30
THE MAILMAN
(*A postás*)   32
UNDERGROUND
(*Underground*)   34
A RUG FOR HOSPITAL STREET
(*Szőnyeg a kolozsvári utcán*)   36
BALLAD ABOUT THE POLICE SEARCH OF OUR HOME
(*Dal a házkutatásról*)   37

I INHABIT YOUR HEART AS A BAT
(*Én lakom szíved mint denevér*) 38
THE LOST TRIBE
(*Az elveszett törzs*) 39
YOU TOO WOULD WATCH YOUR HEAD
(*Kapkodnád fejed*) 41
A POEM ABOUT INFINITE PROGRAMS
(*Vers a végtelen programokról*) 42
DEMON
(*Démon*) 44
THE KOLOZSVÁR HORROR
(*Kolozsvári horror*) 45
THE SAME RIVER
(*Ugyanaz a folyó*) 46
INSTANT PHOTO AT THE MÜNICH RAILROAD STATION
(*gyorsfénykép a müncheni pályaudvaron*) 47
THE POOR RELATION FROM THE WOODS
(*A szegény erdei rokon*) 48
ONE NIGHT IN WALES
(*Egy éjszaka Walesben*) 50
THE POET FROM MEMPHIS
(*A Memphiszből jött költő*) 51
YOUR UMBRELLA
(*Ernyőd...*) 52
FOR MY BIRTHDAY
(*Születésnapomra*) 54
THE KERCHIEF STOLEN UNDER THE GRASS
(*A fű alatt...*) 58
...AND THOSE WHO DIDN'T
(*... és akiket nem*) 60
HUNG OVER
(*Másnap*) 61
BURIAL IN ST. GEORGE
(*Temetés Szentgyörgyön*) 62
WHAT I WANT TO BE WHEN I GROW UP
(*Sztár atyuska rulettje*) 63
WHEN YOU BECOME THE US PRESIDENT
(*majd mikor amerikai elnök leszel*) 64
WHERE THAT FLAPPING COMES FROM
(*Hogy honnan hallom*) 65

I KNOW THIS IS NOT HOW IT GOES
(*Tudom, tudom! Nem úgy mondják*)   66
THE VISIT BY THE SHOCK-WORKERS
(*Az élmunkások látogatása*)   67
YOU DEPARTING IN A RED DOPPLER DRESS
(*Távolodsz vörös Doppler-ruhában*)   68
INDIAN WORDS ON THE RADIO
(*Indián szavak a rádióban*)   69
YOU TAKE A PLANE
(*Gritti a repülőn*)   71
KAFKA AND HIS SISTER STOP IN BUDAPEST ON THEIR WAY
TO LEBANON AND RUN INTO THE ARTIST CSONTVÁRY
(*Kafka és nővére…*)   72
A TALE OF THE BLACK OWL
(*A feketebagoly meséi*)   74
HAPPY YESTERYEAR
(*Kívánok boldog régi évet*)   75
AT HOUDINI'S BIRTHHOUSE IN BUDAPEST
(*Houdini szülőházánál Budapesten*)   76

PART II. LIBERTÉ '56 — Verse excerpts from a drama   79

THE SONG OF A BENEVOLENT DICTATOR
(*Kádár János dala*)   81
EPITAPH
(*Sírfelirat*)   82
PRAYER FOR THE FALLEN HEROES (SONG OF A CLERGYMAN)
(*Ima az elesettekért*)   83
IMRE NAGY: THE PRIME MINISTER'S SONG
(*Nagy Imre: A miniszterelnök dala*)   84
KATINKA: GRANDFATHER'S SONG
(*Katinka: Nagyapa dala*)   85
PRINCE WORONIECZKI'S BALLAD
(*Woronieczki herceg balladája*)   86
PAVEL'S SONG ABOUT CONTINUITY
(*Pável dala az én folytonosságáról*)   87
PAVEL'S PRAYER
(*Pável imája*)   88

NARRATOR: THE MORAL. ABOUT MORTALS.
(Narrátor: *Tanulság. A halandókról.*)   89
SUSAN'S FUNERAL SONG
(*Susan gyászdala*)   90
THE IMAGE OF GOD, OR ELSE THE PRESENT AS THE SUBJECT
OF A CONTRACT BETWEEN THE PAST AND THE FUTURE
(*Istenkép, avagy a jelen, mint a múlt és jövő közti szerződés tárgya*) 91
BALLAD OF JANTSI PEG LEG
(*Ballada Falábú Jancsiról*)   94
TWO SCENES FROM THE DRAMA LIBERTÉ '56   96
    SCENE 85.—About Past Selection   96
    SCENE 123.—The Bureau of Forgotten Things   99

BIOGRAPHICAL NOTES   101
ADDENDA (Géza Szőcs: Letter to Ms. Gloria Steinem)   104
A Note on Transylvanian History   112

Prologue

Playful lexicon with a dada undertone that emphasizes quality of life over art by using art to focus attention on the absurd behavior of the power structure? Yes, this is Géza Szőcs. Imaginative language with a dusting of the surreal characterizes *Liberty, Rats and Sandpaper*. Even the title of his book effectively irritates the senses and evokes sarcastic emotions. His sensibility is terrestrial, not sentimentally celestial. Szőcs understands that allowing abstract gods and flawed humans to make important life decisions risks leading civilizations down one garden path or another. Flawed deities are created by flawed humans, and Szőcs recognizes this irony:

> Rain can see itself grow through snow
> as its mirror-mask in the sod
> the way weeds can penetrate
> the dentures of a buried god.

He also pulls no punches when it comes to demystifying demagogues:

> when you become the u.s. president
> and with golden water pistols in your pocket
> you play cops-and-robbers by yourself
> in the corridors of the white house

Welcome to *Liberty, Rats and Sandpaper*, an intelligent journey through the psyche of one of Hungary's most innovative and outspoken poets. This book by Géza Szőcs deserves the international attention that it is finally receiving.

Alan Britt, Poet
Lost Among the Hours
Towson University, 2016

PART I.
SELECTED POEMS

THE GREAT MARINETTI CAR
(*A nagy Marinetti autó*)

Take a look outside, at the motor car standing by the gate under
a crimson tarp; it's decorated with great exhaust pipes that come
snaking out swollen by the explosions they exhale; this howling
automobile flies like an artillery barrage, and in beauty it surpasses the
Winged Victory of Samothrace; the imaginary extension of its steering
column shoots right through the planet, even through the laps of its
earthly racing course. It's in this car that I'll take you for a ride.

*

 Get your coat, I'm here for you.

Take a look outside, at the motor car standing by the gate under
a crimson tarp; it's decorated with great exhaust pipes that come
snaking out swollen by the explosions they exhale; this howling
automobile flies like an artillery barrage, and in beauty it surpasses
the Winged Victory of Samothrace; the imaginary extension of its
steering column shoots right through the planet, even through the
laps of its earthly racing course, and now in this automobile I'm
taking you for a ride.

*

My dear! Dear, oh dear! Don't look outside. Turn your head away,
don't look under the crimson tarp; I don't want you to see what
remains—alas!—of the motor car decorated with thick exhaust
pipes snaking out swollen by the explosions they exhale, this
howling automobile that used to fly like an artillery barrage,

13

and in beauty it surpassed the Winged Victory of Samothrace, the imaginary extension of its steering column shot right through the planet, even through the laps of its earthly racing course; in this car once I wanted to take you for a ride.

1975

(*Filippo Tommaso Marinetti, Italian poet, invented the aesthetic movement of Futurism after a minor car crash in 1908; one motto he proclaimed: "A speeding automobile is more beautiful than the Winged Victory of Samothrace". The description of the car paraphrases fragments from the* Futurist Manifesto. *Translator's note.*)

LIBERTY, RATS AND SANDPAPER
(*Szabadság...*)

Or the Computer Remembers Donka Simo For the Survivors
of the Underground

> *"Who's unfrayed by the Big Bad Wolf?"*
> *(Donka Simo's telegram)*

The computer puts on airs
because it's learning to ski and laugh
beside searching
       its memory
for a possible
       overlap.
Even a mammoth will
finally go gaga
and fill up slowly
   with tearful sap.

Punch cards. Machine-memory.
Shrapnel: ground-up gold.
It was a flashlight. Or glory.

Wave-grave. Bronze whale bust.
One prisoner? Two if you must.

Liberty. Rats. Sandpaper.

Fliers. Coloratura.
Celtic Bards. Sewing-machine landlords.
Desktop press. Weddings.
And the tricolor violin chords.

Coronary,
      coronations.
Arteries. *Morts. Vivants.* Libations.
Situation-song. Brambleberry.
Military courts. Poet passports.

Provincial town. Provincial Square.

Forget its name … ? Impossible for me.
A deer's making a racket in my memory,
or a gas burner's flame. Fall wind flute.
No such birth recorded in Town Hall.
The Donka name
      does not compute.
Donka. The poor fellow insane?
How's that? How come? Please, explain!

The Simo family. On Provincial Square.
BUT WHAT DID HE WANT? AND
      WHY DID HE CARE?

                                        1985

THE SHIP PROPELLER
(*A hajócsavar*)

I don't know what you'd do with it if I gave you a ship propeller. Let's say, I go deeply into debt, auction off everything I own until I finally manage to get hold of the propeller of an old, weather-beaten ocean liner. On that day when the delivery men drop off the huge ship propeller reeking of the characteristic smell of ship propellers in front of your house and ring the bell, I'll be watching your face from a well-disguised hiding place.

I want a girl who'd be happy with the ship propeller.

1975

A FOUNDLING AMONG EBONY TREES
(*Talált gyerek az ébenfák közt*)

What's this surgery you pursue!
's that you calling me? from under the scalpel:
are you here! you're here, aren't you?

how you lounge on the table!
Naked, like children at dawn
in a garden of ebony fable:

children watched by the laser faces
of wordless adults
behind debating seagull cries
while above them the flapping of wings
turns dark and petrifies.

But as the shadow scampers up
on your pulse for an inner ladder:
in your chest the blood telegraph
goes tap-tap,
reminding you of me,
a hail storm wrecks the ebony park,
goes tap-tap, reminding you of me

and a fist-sized red squirrel quakes
under the black branches of ebony.

1978

THE UNDERGROUND BIRD-WATCHING BLIND
(*A mélyrétegek*)

Someone visited my yard last night
leaving a spade and a pair of wings behind,
and now a downpour licks the toppled
underground bird-watching blind.

The naked skeleton of
a lost angel who once eloped
is phosphorescing there
in groundwater soaked!

Rain can see itself grow through snow
as its mirror-mask in the sod
the way weeds can penetrate
the dentures of a buried god.

1978

THE BAGPIPER
(*A dudás*)

His work done, the bagpiper
wends his way home evening time.
Tattered, filthy, reeking of smoke
and splattered with blood.
The taste of mother's milk wells up in his mouth,
and a flood of dialects, mother-tongue, chirps,
       and Mongol hordes inflects his lips.
"Same thing today" asks the missus.
"Same thing today" nods the exhausted piper.
And then he adds:
I'd like to be life-size.
I'd like to have lotus for supper.
With Paradise for garnish.
Give me a bath. Look at me. It's snowing.
Give me a bath. *Love me. Lave-moi.*

                     1987

TO THE FOREST LODGE, WHEN?
(*Az erdőházba, mikor?*)

On the trout's table the red cauliflower
of spies is dwindling and so is
the blue supper of intelligence officers.
In our shoulders white bone cancer
hovers, flapping its wings.

On our ankles
    the sagging raggedy socks
of the swollen raven glows.
When? What time?
    Have our forests been all used up?
Didn't I hear a raven speak?
    No more forests?
        only forest fires?
            la femme?

cherchez la memoire?
how come no?
definitely no?
how come

                  1977

THE TWENTY-THIRD SNOWFALL
(*A huszonharmadik hóhullás*)

This here around me is my twenty-third snowfall.
A trope of modern lyric poetry, snowfall.

But we didn't even know each other back then!

Listen to this:
if I put together all your first days of snow
they would make up several weeks,
maybe a month. Wouldn't it be fun
to relive that month all in one stretch,
every day of the first snow,
from every year of your life, one after another,—
that month,
even if it's not mine, not at all.
That's why now you should spend it with me.
We could be traveling, week after week
we'd be on the road. One afternoon you'd
look up: WHAT'S THAT? THAT NOISE?—oh, nothing—I'd reply—
nothing special. Machine-fun fire from beyond the woods.

1976

THE REBELS' SUPPER
(*A forradalmárok vacsorája*)

For TGM

On the table hawk paté, water-lily sauté and cake,
lichen torte and a light moss wine and artichoke.

But the dining room is empty. That's when
on your spine a rebel starts to rise with a cherry-
cutting bird inside his chest.

And on the table the scientific bread's on fire and in the attic
wind geese and wind gander gaggle. In the dried-up plumbing
a cuckoo bird mumbles and if you turn on the faucet
snow-yellow grass and cuckoo bones flow out of it.

Oh you, you rebel! Over your head are clacking
steel-flavored apricots.

Indoors it's the howl of spiders
and the wild-boar poppy stuck in the hourglass!
watch it, watch it, the head cuckoo screams!

and outdoors the rebels sprinting spring-style

in the city people are squatting around the cast-iron stallion.
Tar seeps from their eye sockets turned toward the fire,
and the whole city echoes the rolling of torn-off
statue heads carried by the river stream.

THE REBELS GO HOME AND TAKE THE CARBINES OUT
OF THE GREASE-CASE, WIPE THEM OFF, SHINE AND AS-
SEMBLE THEM, THEY WASH THEMSELVES WITH GRASS,
EAT THEIR SUPPERS, COCK THEIR HAND GRENADES
AND GET MOVING.

1975

23

(unfinished)
(*befejezetlen*)

I can hear trees take root on
the other side of the Globe

like I can hear wild roses grow whisperings
and whispers put on night's black robe,

I can even hear water invade
your footprints in the sandy shore.

Someone walks on water in me,
water wheezes on the rose,
and seawater takes a bath in the sea,

I can feel the ocean's heartbeat:
in your wrist I feel it pulsate,
the sea sends waves above the rose,
either that
        or a mountain lake
but I can't help hearing a faint voice speak of
       a sunken island deep inside you,
he sounds like a city nerd I know,
   his voice is full of dread,
as if he didn't want it heard.

1977

DRESS UP YOUR INNER TEDDY BEAR
(Add rá a benned alvó gyanútlan kisgyerekre)

This verse is a grass-green yarn
you may decide to disperse
and spin again as you darn

this verse is a piece of cloth
the floods keep on weaving
and tearing apart again

it has a grass-green glow
with sky-blue slipping through

the wind fetches a cloud
and finally puts it on you:

this verse is but a shawl
to wear around the shoulders.

You feel him sleeping inside
like an inner teddy bear.
Dress him in this verse; it'll keep
him warm and dispel his despair,

put it on that unsuspecting
little child sleeping inside,
tossing and turning all day
and all night, too tired to hide.

1978

25

EVENING PRAYER
(*Esti ima*)

God, let huge oceans have their birth,
  and the greenest grasses too on earth!

  where there was but swampy ice,
  let there be now wide blue skies,

when the moon climbs way up there
let the clouds ignite the air!

  your hands have managed to create
  so many houses to this date,

now let Kolozsvár and Budapest *abide*
  there by the riverside!

  paint our eyes in lively colors,
give us bodies to fit our collars

  and give us names, God, if you can,
  because we lack them, woman or man,

  make of us, we ask, our Lord,
brothers now of one accord,

  let us be Máté and Gigi,
but not different mothers' progeny,

  may our Erdély, the beauteous,
  be the mother to all of us!

like a gentle breeze descends
    to our faces and hair's ends,

    let divine hands also tease us,
stick around here, our Jesus,

    it's His visit that we celebrate,
      that He sits here with a plate

    even though to mortal eyes
He can't be seen in any guise,

    yet in whole now here He stands
but not to our groping hands,

not except over a pound
    is His Presence to be found:

His steps can light up any lake
as clear as four and four stand in eight.

Our Father, every minute on our tether
    the dentures of destruction snap together
but you keep us resurrected and alert
    when you button up our lives around us
    like a warm and ample winter shirt—

    God, we thank you for everything;
      and if you were to hide someday
        in eternity's banned bay,
      in painted pictures on church walls,
        in carved cold stone in closed-off stalls:

Our Father, we now ask you
let us come again upon you
in a cornfield,
or, who cares?
in the fields of
our own prayers
or in Emontekiő.

1983

WINTER SONNET
(*Téli szonett*)

Bounced by the long-distance train I am
in a child's hands, a rattle or a raggedy
doll, while hardship may be lashing others,
no wonder some people envy me,

and how is she getting on? Shivering,
I'm sure she's shivering in this monstrous cold
that breaks open gypsy-moth cocoons,
their bare death-fright is something to behold;

she spends her day play-acting, puts on
and takes off her face, combs her flaxen hair
lingering in front of the mirror
before putting herself in sleep's care.

In my mouth a glass tongue tinkles, and I
sport a pair of glass ears and a single green-glass eye.

I'll have to decide by the end of the year.
One way or the other. But what about?
A voice inside me keeps urging me to decide by the end of the year,
but I have no idea what it is about.
I'm afraid I may not find out before the end of the year, and then they will
assume I will have decided thus and so—even though there was no decision,
no alternative has presented itself.
What's going to come of this?

1977

LISTENING TO MUHAMMAD ALI
(*Muhammad Ali két verse*)

1. The Photograph of Rain

The wind is fierce, it messes up
our words,
I shut myself up in the house
with a photo of rain
and sing of the ships
that brought my ancestors to
the plantations
sing of power and jazz and
the behemoth who fills up
my mirror and wears
my suits.

Oh, how tough I was
and how my flexed body
was tanned by the stares
that tossed so many
bouquets in the ring,
how tough I was
and how much I fear
that boy
sitting alone in the house
with a few sips of water
in the palm of his hand
supposedly a photo of rain.

2. *Ars Poetica*

I'm writing poems now
I'm writing so as to give my right hand something
else to clutch beside a gun
so that we may all love one another
and be set free.

1974

(*Géza Szőcs's interest in Muhammad Ali's personality and story compelled him to write several poems in the famous boxer's style; the above poem is a good example. Translator's note.*)

THE MAILMAN
(*A postás*)

On February eleventh
the postman rings
    (…aha, when it was an apple!)
He sings, you hear the postman.
But it's hard
to make
out the song
when was it
indeed
when you were
once so:
very young.

The forbidden apple is
stalked by the arm,
remembering you
it gives alarm.

Remembrance rises,
staring at you hard: aha,
when it was but …
    when it was but an apple
the girl had stolen
with the guard!

February eleventh.
The snow piles erode, and
a half-a-day of Eden is
your snack for the road.

Inside you now marriage
entraps her song, it's
no longer merry,
no longer so young.

On February eleventh
        or thereabouts
mailmen roam the town
in search of that other one
who is also me
yes I

                1983

UNDERGROUND
(*Underground*)

With the red comb of hemorrhage in my mouth,
all in all in tolerable shape,

yesterday I watched the gravediggers
shovel some bones out with the dirt
by the Házsongárd cemetery gate,

my little girl is crying for the puppet
she has dropped into the well:
the folk songs are changing costumes
into warrants for arrest, to tell,

who knows, what people live down in the well!

Sleepless creature is the guard.
But there's more to it to boot.

*

The helmet flower grows out of the skeleton,
flower in the unoccupied helmet.
Remembrance lives on down below
in the dawn with coal there melted.

With a red comb in his mouth.

My photos he took with them along with my poems:
Colonel, You are a distinguished collector, take this one too,
with the others, Colonel, I don't mind.

Nowhere else will it ever be read
unless—who knows—it may be broadcast
by an often jammed and harassed
faraway radio it may be bled
           and shed
                instead.

                      1983

A RUG FOR HOSPITAL STREET
(*Szőnyeg a kolozsvári utcán*)

For Á. E.

If it's not you
who can weave it
then I will or
someone else

a nurse will who can
weave a rug while
waiting for the
night-time bells

a nurse can weave it
nightly as she
waits and waits on
silent bells

till a feather-
dress grows from the
wails and pains she
never tells

and flying off
she'll cry: your youth
was easy loot

to someone else
as it's told by
all the bells
all the bells

1983

BALLAD ABOUT THE POLICE SEARCH OF OUR HOME
(*Dal a házkutatásról*)

With love to the Kertész family in Nagyvárad

The doorbell rings: who could that be?
The police! let's all get dressed, one-two-three!

  So says Lori, slightly raising the window shade
  in November, Sunday dawn about to break.

Someone shakes loose the pockets of my suit.
Ma, our Sunday dinner has derailed en route.
It's a mob scene out in the street
   —we were departing,
       dear neighbors, it's nice that we meet.
Thus we exchange greetings as we pass.
Colonel, sir, don't forget to turn off the gas.

A local shower, a little soak, so what's the kick?
The summer's gone, and we missed every out-door flick.

1984

I INHABIT YOUR HEART AS A BAT
(*Én lakom szíved mint denevér*)

How many hearts do you have?
I'd like to live in all of them:
even as a Martian breathes*
inside me every now and then.

At dusk, d'you feel how it smarts?
    the smoldering scratches
in your hair and your hearts?

---

*the way he breathes here and avers
mixing all up facts with verse:

even as a Martian breathes
inside me every now and then,
his ears with stethoscope he feeds
and watches Mars in me at night:

there is nothing like it yet
nothing would feel quite so right.

1985

THE LOST TRIBE
(*Az elveszett törzs*)

Poem about the Revolution, dedicated to Hungarians in New York

> "*The name of Kossuth Lajos Street in the town of Marosvásárhely has been changed. The name will be Calarasi Street henceforth.*"
> —*News Report*

"... and cuts like a flower through the blade"
—that's how he speculates—
  "like a volley fired at a protest parade
and Calarasi—that is myself..."
that's how Kossuth speculates in Vásárhely
by the Grand Hotel
        in the Grand Hotel
"and just when the scene is about to fade
        the revolution starts coughing one night
like the lung from the cellar
        or a carburetor
or the way a bundle of kindling wood lights up
the wreckage of an airplane at the bottom of the sea;—
like the grass grows out of the battlefield
grows out choked and burnt away,
he, too, grows up to be carried off
and he, too, grows up and will be carried off
by smallpox or the ship of emigrants—
but then he rears his head in a cafe!
The revolution.
        HO-HO-HO! Or at least the word,
carried by the grass and hearsay,

by the groceries and the battle field,
and you'll catch sight of his coat at a rally
in Budapest
    or New York, in Lupény;
the revolution's coat is one size too big
the revolution
    wears a coat one size too grand
and leans over you in your sleep
with his face and a ragged hand
and he and you
the one unmated shoe
in the moonlight of a hurried murder
he is the phantom cutting through
the occupation
      and its charade:
like a scream cuts through
the silent blade in the night
that's how he cuts through
that's how he cuts through
like a flower through the blade
and a blade then through the night
and he's bilingual like Papa Bem,
in Hungarian
and Polish renowned
and he is indeed the lost tribe
the tribe
    that gets
        lost and
            always found."

                     1984

YOU TOO WOULD WATCH YOUR HEAD
(*Kapkodnád fejed*)

An eagle may fly like this smack
up against your head and all
you feel is the feathers' swish,
and a wing's caressing fall
softly and yet it can tear
your face apart, there's no escape
from the pecking and the claws
and your *inner face* is bare
like a dead king's ripped-up cape

but the smack flies on and on
inside you—ripples a lake—down deep
where *your soul's own mirrors* creep
you feel the bull's-eye throw of dart
thrown by death there playing part
: at a time like this you rightly feel
like a cupboard where the glassware shelf
has collapsed amidst a crashing peal

Waking from the blow dealt by the pest
you question every face around: did any
of them hear the crash inside your chest

1973

A POEM ABOUT INFINITE PROGRAMS
(*Vers a végtelen programokról*)

> *"What a small computer can do with*
> *a large program a large computer can do*
> *with a small program. It stands to reason*
> *that an infinitely large program can operate*
> *on its own, without any computers."*
>
> Stanislaw Lem

Under our love there's another one,
under a program
                        other programs perk,
inside an ogre lives another ogre,
under the law a deeper law's at work—

underground creeks run all through life
behind every star a hundred others lurk:

under our love there's another one.

Livelier, darker and more moist.
Throbbing, it eludes your grasp
and kicks off its blanket at night
like a child having fun.
                        Throws it away.

You'll sip the deeper wine adrift
in your wine, you will some day,

UNDER OUR LOVE THERE'S ANOTHER ONE

and we'll both melt into the infinitely
larger programs' interplay.

1984

DEMON
(*Démon*)

Under your window in shirt sleeves, violin in hand,
the earthquake-youth is on guard, a wheezing yellow beast,
in his double watch-dog heart liquid and slow velvet.

Holding his knife against the demon's throat he stares
at the tracks left by the sleeping stars' cold shoes on the beach.

He finds the soft snaps of your heartbeat with his fingertips and on his way home
—when morning arrives in panic, bringing its hemp rope—
he scrawls these huge letters on your wall with a yellow chalk:
ARE YOU THE SAME? ARE YOU NOT? OR ARE YOU?

Holding the demon by the throat he keeps staring
at the tracks left by the sleeping star's cold shoes on the beach.

1980

THE KOLOZSVÁR HORROR
(*Kolozsvári horror*)

On a November night, worrying about a
police raid on my apartment, I tossed
a cassette tape in the river. Your voice was
on it; you probably know which recording
it was.

For a long time afterwards, every time I
crossed that bridge over the Szamos
I could hear you calling from the water.

1983

*(Kolozsvár—Cluj in Romanian—is a city on the Szamos River in
Transylvania. Translator's note.)*

THE SAME RIVER
(*Ugyanaz a folyó*)

*A song about the impossibility of
stepping into the same river once.*

Standing by the river I recall
a long-ago and mild-mannered fall.

Footsteps in the water, under it.
The bloodshot eyeballs
of the flower-vendor girls
accompany your steps: you tread

on autumn water in the swollen riverbed,
what the river wants though
is to eat your heavy head.

A dizzy spell and down you go,
seeking your old river and your footsteps
somewhere down below.

1983

instant photo at the münich railroad station
(*gyorsfénykép a müncheni pályaudvaron*)

quietly your picture dries on you
while the red light is still lit

and you hear a stifled voice,
scratchy from explaining it:

bitte die fotos trocken lassen
solange rote lampe brennt

slowly you dry on yourself
AS THE RED LIGHT'S SEDIMENT

you get flushed to the roots
and the hair bristles on your back
because you hear inside you
the station master's crack:

LOOK, YOU'VE LEFT YOURSELF AT HOME!

1982

THE POOR RELATION
FROM THE WOODS
(*A szegény erdei rokon*)

I.

1. The poor relation from the woods stands at the door.
2. He has an archaic stare.
3. "...thanks," he mutters bashfully.
4. "...back home? Well... nowadays even the salt...
   what I mean is, not even..."
5. "And the bears, do they still come around?"
6. The relation has an archaic laugh.
7. "Sure enough... they do."
8. "You can have these shoes. They'll help against
   the bears. And we don't need them any more."
9. The poor relation, awkwardly, like a child:
10. "God bless you for your kindness."
11. "Dear, get him some salt, too."
12. "Well, God bless."
13. The relation from the woods departs.
14. "I see they still know how to speak, back there.
15. That's quite something, how well they can... yes, well enough.
16. That they still know how."

II.

Static in the stethoscope.
The leg is kicking, cut off at the knee.
Noise in the listening device,
the horse is silent in the static-storm,
blood is pouring out of the stethoscope
and the wintry sky is shredded into snow.

III.

The relations at the edge of the woods.
Wrinkled and agitated, they're questioning
and asserting something all day long,
saying it and asking it over and over,
but nobody can understand a word they say;
the stars keep blinking but they too get it wrong.

1984

ONE NIGHT IN WALES
(*Egy éjszaka Walesben*)

The sweetest sorrow it is to part in the small towns of Wales
and among the towns inside you it's the Welsh kind that prevails
and should you step outside of yourself, that's what greets
you: farewell alleys encircle your life with parting streets.

Dawn is glowing in the grass, and kisses bend over your lips
but you know the night will not survive the morning.
The blue feet of forget-me-nots hammer on sinking ships.

With the clanking of the train tucked under your tongue you trouble
your mind with: was it her you kissed? Or a departing double?

1984

THE POET FROM MEMPHIS
(*A Memphiszből jött költő*)

Is it true? Not from Transylvania?
The poet ponders his exile
with the contents of a thermos
soaking his head in the Nile,

in green water, fizzing with
cormorant and crocodile.
A pharaoh whispers secret old
predictions he must guard—

how many predictions on the poet's list?
how many asses in Assuan?

The pharaoh cannot find himself.

It may be too late to stem this
old news: our poet is from Memphis.

1992

YOUR UMBRELLA
(*Ernyőd...*)

Your umbrella saves you not.
Who said it would!
A mouse is barking on the roof,
your ears are gone for good.

Your umbrella saves you from
no one. The tide in your chest
cools off and warms while
in the foliage growing ogres nest:

they all grow,
        their atoms and their spume,
the beaks, the wings,
        the hair, the doom,
the bridesmaid
        and the bridegroom.

IN THE HEARTS OF TREES YOU LINGER:

Under the waves the mermaid
strolls on, shaking out her locks,

this defenseless wild beast
in a terminal waterfall

trying to dry out her skirt
in the tide of the squall

while bears are chasing each
other among the trees—

Your umbrella saves you not. Who
said life would be a breeze.

1988

FOR MY BIRTHDAY
(*Születésnapomra*)

Today I, too, am 32.
And how many more to go?
only the densely dark math
of the night may know.

God hovers between being and nothingness
but it's in rubber balls he must exist.
The rubber truncheon's restless sleep
invokes my picture from the mist:

the rubber truncheon is at rest
    and so is social consciousness:
no more alienation for today.

The spirit essence of this poem
shines in perfect rhymes.
Moral eclipse often slips past us
at nocturnal times.

In your eyes, dear, the grass is
overshadowed by a tree:
your sight is governed by the grass
and fear's geometry.

The solar eclipse on a dark
parachute slips down in the park.
But there arises
      in the math books
another kind of space;

with wider perspectives
and kinder expletives
without martyrs and
dotted by all spring days.

Seven years ago I said:
I DON'T WANT MY LETTERS CENSORED BY THE GUARD
AND THE PRISON WALL TO BE SO THICK AND HARD
BUT I DO WANT A BREACH BETWEEN THE EVENTS OF LIFE
WHERE A HAND CAN SLIP THROUGH WITH A KNIFE.

And five or six years ago
I didn't yield up my life
on a battlefield
the blood of youth did not drain from my heart.
But the person who used to adore
me then
now loves me no more
and my mail is censored by the guard,
the prison walls are still thick and hard,
and there's no breach between the events of life
for a hand to slip through with
                    a knife
but someday
the wall
with its bricks
will have to fall
and a telescope
will be there
wrapped in a densely typed
questionnaire:

Nationality:
  Csángó-Egyptian,
  and partly Volga-German;
  my mother was Coptic,
    and my father Csángó.

Where would you like to emigrate:
  I could say—if I'm allowed a cliché—
    let's say into the future I would go;
  or I could live in the past;
    and if possible,
        in the present as well.
  But it doesn't matter where and when and how much—

Offense against OUR STATE:
  In Orwell's words: thought-crime.

Citizenship:
  The grammar of liberty
  the air of liberty!
    whoever whiffs this air
  can never live on it
  again, or of it free,

  wide awake he lives,
  deprived
    of dreams,
  and target-shoots,
  new grammar
    he schemes,

or else he's out to scan the skies
for a star-encrusted phrase
that he senses will soon rise
from the shadows in a blaze.

He speaks to those who
hope for better things
   and trust in what the poet ... sings.

                          1985

(The Csángó people are a smaller Hungarian-speaking group living in their traditional ways far apart from the mainstream Hungarian population. Translator's note.)

THE KERCHIEF STOLEN UNDER THE GRASS
(A fű alatt…)

Light bulbs, night bulbs,
light up on the telephone pole.
The garden gate is left ajar.
I shut my eyes though like a mole.

Too much light,
    much too much of it.
Don't look at me or say a word.
WHO GOES THERE
    and why turn on the lights?
or no one? only garden dragons:
red cabbage heads
    and other spring delights?
Lying flat in the green garden
a corpse
    a pilot now long dead
adding and dividing with the hurt
for how long now oh-oh
                for how long
will the clock keep ticking
forgotten in the dirt?

The fevered lamp pole cannot cease
to sprinkle its light to the trees.
The pilot-face lies in the grass.
Fixing the silk camisole
disgrace is getting dressed.

My-god, what's growing in my tummy?
Nothing but a cabbage head.
Beyond the brook I left my skirt;

or did it get stolen from the fest?
and that's why it is turning black,
someone must have got it hexed?
The clock is silent in the dirt,
the ditty's silent on the tongue:
Brussels sprouts,
a pair of boobies sprout,
girlie, girlie greets

the girlie of the streets.

1984

... AND THOSE WHO DIDN'T
(*... és akiket nem*)

1. No one was required to partake of the lotus.
2. It was only to one's advantage to do so.
3. Those who didn't were looked upon with suspicion.
4. And, of course, there was nothing else to eat.
5. So more and more died of moral shock.
6. The lotus stew was in great demand.
7. And so was the cheap lotus brandy, especially
  by the morally naked.
8. Oblivion, the old underground sin, raised its
  head above the grass.
9. In the cafeteria there was one person who
  pushed the lotus plate away.
10. By then no one paid attention to him.
11. "Moral midgets,"
  he muttered to himself,
  "marked themselves with mortal birth defects."

1986

HUNG OVER
(*Másnap*)

And then comes the next day.
Time to sow the seeds
and then to reap except the crop
is someone else's thing
the hour of parting is on hand
but first that of the offering.

Nothing will now upset
the system's circling except
the tap-tap of a crutch and
the tissues your tears have kept.

Out there on the road is Peg Leg.
A raven from above beholds a glow:
The sparkles on the rusty coat
of departure in the snow.

1983

BURIAL IN ST. GEORGE
(*Temetés Szentgyörgyön*)

Man is but a P.O. Box
and the letter inside is his soul.
A song is heard: the underworld
extends to life a new parole.

Sight though cannot play
its role until it hits the next
vision, the one to the bottom of
the optic nerve recessed.

Backing up you go forward
all the way to the water gap
where the eyes close and
the envelope then flips its flap.

When man is ushered into
the halls of the underworld
God scans the letter after
it becomes unfurled.

Man is but a funny creature!
As he takes his death to dance,
his life, like a briefcase,
slips forgotten from his hands.

*

THE BODY NESTLES IN THE GRAVE.
WHILE OTHERS STEAL THE SOUL
A GALLOPING HORSE, OFFERING
ITS BACK, RESCUES THE AUREOLE.

1990

WHAT I WANT TO BE WHEN I GROW UP
(*Sztár atyuska rulettje*)
(Fragment)

*Dedicated to my grandfather's bronze bust that was melted down
with others after the war for the casting of a large statue of Stalin*

In unknown boots
the unknown soldier
always starts marching toward a well-defined target:
not again and again
but continuously.

When I grow big, when I grow even bigger:
I want to be an unknown soldier.

Just like that.
But also a monument,
continuity cast in bronze.

You'd all love the unknown in me.

You'd bring me flowers instead of hot soup!

You ladies, you my ladies.
On your tables my future supper is getting cold;
while in your bed my body's imprint keeps tossing and turning
I'll be gaping at you with bronze eyes and lips.

1988

when you become the US president
(majd mikor amerikai elnök leszel)

when you become the US president
and with golden water pistols in your pocket
you play cops-and-robbers by yourself
in the corridors of the white house
or else you walk outside to stand on the democratic demarcation line
or walk out to stand on the dividing line or the continental divide
and you drink a cocktail of nitric and hydrochloric acids that separates
      base metals from gold,
when you separate evil from good
and the useless from the useful:
one imperceptible move and you can't tell
if you've stepped over the hill
to the other side of your life
or you are still here

       *

the great divide and the purifying acid cocktail,
you're past the halftime

you'll play hide and seek
and bury the black box containing your last words
in the basement of the white house,
you'll be digging in the basement of the white house
with a computer crucifix on your forehead, wearing galoshes
and the hot line twisted around your neck,
when you become the u.s. or the russian president.

           1988

WHERE THAT FLAPPING COMES FROM
(Hogy honnan hallom)

In a hotel room in Mexico,
remember? I got the news you were
staying there like any other witch,
wearing green elastic shoes.

And from your room the rustling
of your constant restlessness:
the swish of your skirt and whale-skin
jacket when you started to undress!

As your keyhole was to show
there wasn't much room for your wings
in your bed in Mexico.

Then I locked the door on you
and boarded up the window frames,
you still managed to fly off and
by the morning you were no more.

Ever since then I've been eavesdropping
in hotel corridors in search of
your hidden phonograph
that sends out a flapping sound at night
along with your sobs and laugh.

1990

I KNOW THIS IS NOT HOW IT GOES
(*Tudom, tudom! Nem úgy mondják*)

> The wine in the bottle reflects the events of
> its earlier life such as blooming and fermenting
> as if it could remember. The wine in the bottle.

A huge thrashing machine is roaming the countryside
it's time to thrash the grapes and tomatoes
I am the memory of wine
    its attic and its shutters
from behind the slats I can see you bloom
    and it makes me dizzy like
riesling and fiddling in the spring
how elegant you are
like a barefoot tulip stem.

      *

High-test gas turns opaque
at the corner filling station,
algae grow over my heart,
from the gas pump a trout barks.
Cyanide and money change hands.
The flea market is open back home.
Time to harvest and thrash the grapes.

              1982

THE VISIT BY THE SHOCK-WORKERS
(*Az élmunkások látogatása*)

One morning you awake faced by a bunch of tear-soaked men.
On the elevator of your possessions they step into your life,
with predatory looks they sink into it,
                    these predators;
however your faithful yesterdays bounce them out,
they land on the shore gaping like serialized gnashing,
                    or like seals,
or like a saw,
or like rain-soaked farmhands, mining engineers.

Out in the backyard children are playing doctors,
mommy and daddy, the bully and the raid leader.
They bawl out proudly:
when I grow up
I want to be a henchman like daddy!
                                1983

67

YOU DEPARTING
IN A RED DOPPLER DRESS
(*Távolodsz vörös Doppler-ruhában*)

Why is your voice so deep?
How come those angora eyes? Did you get a sunburn?
You keep running away from me?
Or is it only your dress that's red?
The world headed for a U-turn?
Will you start loving me again?
And come back to me in a blue dress, your hair dyed blue?

1980

INDIAN WORDS ON THE RADIO
(*Indián szavak a rádióban*)

To poet William Least Heat Moon

The Indians of the prairie will not let us down.
Others yes, but not them, they will not let us down.

Had they known what was to take place at Segesvár
—but they knew not what was to take place at Segesvár—
surely they would have shown up too,
some would have known they were coming too:
Papa Bem, the Indians are coming, they would have said,
one morning to Papa Bem this they would have said:

across the Bering Strait
across the Bering Strait
an Indian cavalry is on its way,
cutting across Siberia
cutting its way to us
it's coming to our aid—

the valiant officers would have talked like this,
tossing their gold-braided hats up in the air.

My Indian brother, we haven't even got a reservation.
Ghetto, bantustan, a reservation
sometimes would be fine with us, but we have none.
The tribe gets together in the cafe,
we stand around a lot in the cafe.
Miss, don't spare that Indian pie.
That's what we say but to ourselves we think
but to ourselves we actually think:

some day a few Indians
across the Bering Strait
across any kind of strait
will cut their way through to us
to come to our aid
to come to our aid.

The Indians do not let anybody down.
The Indians will not let us down.

1985

(*In order to understand the dedication and the poem itself the reader should know that at the Nov. 15th, 1985 session of the Cultural Forum in Budapest William Least Heat Moon, a Native American writer and a member of the US delegation gave a detailed report on Géza Szőcs's predicament. He passed on the following information to the conference: Géza Szőcs is under house arrest, and the policeman watching the house has orders to tear the paper out of the typewriter if the poet should ever sit down to it. Mr. Least Heat Moon appealed to the Romanian government to regard poets as a national treasure, and he also called upon all those present to make public the names of writers condemned to silence anywhere the delegates may travel... Géza Szőcs was informed of the above by friends who had been following the proceedings of the Cultural Forum on the radio: that is why the reference to the radio in the title.*

The revolution hinted at took place in 1848 against Hapsburg rule and was defeated in the battle of Segesvár; "Papa" Bem was a popular general of Polish origin. Also, Seklers see themselves as the native Hungarian population overrun by the Romanian majority much like the Native American Indians were dispossessed by the white settlers; thus identification with oppressed peoples of the world was a natural outcome of this situation which was also exacerbated by Ceausescu's brutal communist dictatorship at that time.

This long footnote is the accumulation of comments by various publishers; only the last paragraph is by the translator.)

YOU TAKE A PLANE
(*Gritti a repülőn*)

Who gets to weave your hair?

The sea goes to sleep at Xmas
only one eye of the storm
       left wide open,
and the angels keep looking for
their topcoats in the tide.

The water takes a bath in its past
like Santa in his blood sugar.

The sea falls asleep the same night
with only one eye open wide, showers run
across it; only the green light blinks
below the surface, flushed with pride.

you're taking a plane to get here

the level of the ocean rises and ebbs
with the blood-sugar count.

Blood meanders through its sieves
like winter wind through weaving looms.

You're on a plane but your wet
mouth burrows through the ocean.

1988

71

KAFKA AND HIS SISTER
STOP IN BUDAPEST ON THEIR WAY TO
LEBANON AND RUN INTO
THE ARTIST CSONTVÁRY
(*Kafka és nővére…*)
(Fragment)

In another life I am a carnelian,
a flesh-colored precious stone.
A girl loses me in a ballroom and
since then I don't know if I exist.
That's why I became a fireman
on a steam locomotive to Lebanon.
I had inheritance in that land
a giant cedar tree I'd won.

       *

Another life
another spring
from the tree a
leaf takes its leave

but the carnelian
and the carnival
were not just mere
    make believe

when at the station
a pretty young lady
stepped off
the express train

losing me
forever and
never to
hold me again

*

"Say, don't you ever worry about waking up one morning as a giant
           cockroach?"
"No. I usually wake up with the feeling I must save the world."

*

So that's what went on at the ball

I had an inheritance in Lebanon,
the precious stone flaming in the tree
because we feed the boiler
with the cedar of certainty.

*

Two gentlemen and a lady go up to this kid
loafing at the railroad station and ask him:
Do you think there is a God? The kid says:
God is not just anybody *who may or may not exist.*

1990

A TALE OF THE BLACK OWL
(*A feketebagoly meséi*)

A dragonfly alighted on a branch of a sequoia sapling, a tree still very young and—in spite of belonging to a species noted for their size and longevity—not taller than a mouse standing upright on hind legs.

"Watch it," the sequoia hissed, "you're going to break off my branches."

"So what?" the dragonfly gave the offhand answer. "No one lives forever."

"Maybe not forever," mumbled the potentially giant fir, "but possibly for a long, long time. And that's what I'm hoping for."

"Just how long?" the dragonfly sneered. "Ten days? Or even longer? For five hundred days?"

The fir tree was silent. Perhaps doing a quick calculation.

"Life lasts only for one day." The dragonfly went on, thinking out loud. "But it has to be lived, it must be lived, in such a way as if a life of ten thousand years was crammed into it, that's the way it must be lived. Good Heavens! How could I take it, living five or six days long, getting ugly, wrinkled and wretched?" The dragonfly asked aghast.

"Cramming ten thousand years into one day?" The fir tree thought it over: And my fear is, that after living for twenty thousand years, my life will perhaps seem to me no longer than one short, fleeting day.

(*From* Limpopo,
a novel published in 2007)

Part I. Selected Poems

HAPPY YESTERYEAR
(*Kívánok boldog régi évet*)

To the past the eyes now veer
So I wish you happy yesteryear

I wish you could relive the past
As you have it in your memory cast

As if you understood yesterday
And all that it had to give away

Your happy old self was given to cheer
This now passing, passed-out old year
In which it dwelt for 12 long months

As the tenant signed on the lease:
Your self like a fish or a soul at ease

Or like some star up in the sky
Swimming free like fish in water
It leaped over the year on the fly

Receiving all you held dear

To the last year now say goodbye
And open a window to the new year

December 31, 2015

AT HOUDINI'S BIRTHHOUSE IN BUDAPEST
(*Houdini szülőházánál Budapesten*)

I. Airport among Mountain Peaks
From a Sherpa's notes

Landing strips, glaciers.
The guru is about to go,
to fly up into even higher skies
although still stumbling in snow.

The guru's plane is taxiing
among glaciers, clouds and lava.

They look up to—him among the stars—
the mute people of Himalaya.

II. Conversation with the Escape Artist
To David Merlini

"You've escaped from quite a few traps, haven't you, oh magician of magicians?"
"That's right, just like you said, my mortal friend."

"That means from your body, too."
"That's right. And after that from matter, too, somehow."

"Matter is a very dark cage, isn't it, Master?"
"I've almost forgotten what it was like, my mortal friend."

76

"And what happened to you after you'd slipped out of your body
like from a straightjacket and stepped out of matter, too, Master?"

"Imagine a house. That's the body. If you can get out of it, you're still
locked in the middle of a large estate. Surrounded by impenetrable walls."

"That's no other than matter itself, isn't it? But you freed yourself from that, too."
"Yes, I succeeded in getting out of there. To find myself in a forest."

"And then?"
"After that I wiggled out of there, too, and then moved on and on …
That's how I reached the Highest Garden."

"The one not made of matter."
"The one separated from matter by five levels. It's five levels above."

"And now? Where are you now, oh Master of Masters?"
"Where else but inside you, my mortal friend."

2017

Verse excerpts from a drama about
the 1956 Uprising in Hungary against
the Soviet dictatorship; the drama
was published in 2005 and produced
in 2006 in Debrecen, Hungary.

THE SONG
OF A BENEVOLENT DICTATOR
(*Kádár János dala*)

Didn't they like the split-pea soup?
didn't they get their fill of beer?

wasn't the kasha quite enough?
wasn't the concrete flat a gift to cheer?

Why is this shiftless, lazy,
bow-legged, ungrateful mob

always stirring up some trouble and
then call on their buddy God?

They'll hang from János Kádár trees
singing of God's mysteries!

You beasts of pre-fab concrete flats!
didn't you like the split-pea soup?

They will hang from my gallows with
their God's neck in the same big loop.

My prrrroletarian fist will strike them dead!

EPITAPH
(*Sírfelirat*)

Don't bury me in Kremlin's wall,
don't you make me seem so rude.

From that wall Peg Leg's peg leg
would most certainly protrude.

PRAYER FOR THE FALLEN HEROES (SONG OF A CLERGYMAN)
(*Ima az elesettekért*)

Lord who saw them
      facing volleys of machine-gun fire
      in the wide avenues
You saw their hearts too
      and knew they were
      looking for You
with a carbine on the shoulder and
      classroom notes in their pockets:
You know and measure all things,
You see through the dark, my Lord,
and hear what's inaudible
      to human ear,
You know how they felt getting on the tram
      or seeing mulberry bloom
      or in the morning fresh snow appear,
what happened to them is an open book to You,
and You know they volunteered their lives for

their loved ones
and although the mourning will never end,
look, the prayer runs out.
Falls silent. Still. Finished.
      It's come to an end.
Now we bury them in the ground,
but on the third day they will rise again
and turn into angels in heaven.

IMRE NAGY: THE PRIME MINISTER'S SONG
(*Nagy Imre: A miniszterelnök dala*)

One day he'll come in disguise,
he hasn't got an overcoat,
from his grave God will rise
and bring us a life-saving boat.

You rebellious young lads,
you heroes of no fame—
does God redeem even those
he doesn't know by name?

You eternal revolutions,
you holy rebellions!
Haven't Hungarians on earth
numbered hundreds of millions?

And how many more are bound
to be born singing a new song?
Standing by your cradle are
Magyar poets, old and young.

KATINKA: GRANDFATHER'S SONG
(*Katinka: Nagyapa dala*)

When my granddad took me to the Grand Circus,
when he took me to the zoo,

every giraffe and every lion,
every fox and every kangaroo,

and every clown, every fire-eater, sword-eater, snake-charmer,
and ventriloquist and knife-thrower and tightrope walker
and strongman and every elephant
waved to him and offered him their hands,
their feet, hooves or paws

and trunks and said: you can count on us too,
yes, count on us too, we will be there Mister Comrade President,
                    we will be there Mister President.

PRINCE WORONIECZKI'S BALLAD
(*Woronieczki herceg balladája*)

Where can my sword, my pistol be?
Caught in a horseless cavalry.

I see no father in the Tsar,
Nick's no big daddy to me.

I take no orders from Moscow—

listen to me, listen you guard!
You can grind your wolf teeth hard…

Once I was Prince Woronieczki:
you'll get a dead smile from me.

*

Where's my rifle, where's my steed!
On my body worms will feed.
If I only had a lance!
I'd be back in Poland in no time,
fog would fetch my travel plans.

Heavenly tunes, unearthly lights,
the gravediggers busy throng,
all are waiting just for me.
I've come to the end of my song.

Where could my horses be?
Who said life was much too long.

PAVEL'S SONG ABOUT CONTINUITY
(Pável dala az én folytonosságáról)

Now you see it, now you don't.
Nothing's there, yet something to see.
You the key? And what's the lock?
You the lock? And what's the key?

An unfit lock will never give
memories a chance to live.
Maybe looking for some help
your window's looking through itself.

PAVEL'S PRAYER
(*Pável imája*)

God, prepare a past for me
that would let me be just me,
that you could run over every night, holding my hand
and bathing me in continuity
among those who are also me.

God, dress me up with my wings,
God, prepare my death.
… as I surmise, was it fate?
or the fabric sown between
its strands? And was the future
in no way to be foreseen?
Speak to chansons in chansons,
but it'll do no good, no good at all…

NARRATOR: The Moral. About Mortals.
(*Narrátor: Tanulság. A halandókról.*)

You may try and exchange your life
for another of a brighter tone:
but you can't, because free will
is a captive of its own.

You cannot win over fate:

you'll also exchange yourself
if you exchange your fated life.
Simple days belong alone
to the field surgeon and his knife.

SUSAN'S FUNERAL SONG
(*Susan gyászdala*)

Did you hear your lover's tongue?
or a balalaika song?
The blood, the blood. So crimson dark.
Though it can be used for paint,
it can be spilt, pumped and applied.

Did you hear you lover's tongue?
or a balalaika song?

But that's how it is with love.
It floods you in an endless tide,
can't be measured
             can't be explained.
It lives on, never to go faint.
Did you hear your lover's tongue?
or a balalaika song?

THE IMAGE OF GOD, OR ELSE THE PRESENT AS THE SUBJECT OF A CONTRACT BETWEEN THE PAST AND THE FUTURE

(Istenkép, avagy a jelen, mint a múlt és jövő közti szerződés tárgya)

> *Everything that exists is also the germ of that which it will become. IV. 36.*
> *He who can see the present has seen it all, all that has ever existed or will exist. VI. 31.*
> *Marcus Aurelius:* Meditations

Always shows up in disguise;
for overcoat he wears a nod,
he comes in secret to visit us,
and that visitor is God.

His image has an aura like
memory does by sea possessed:
our image belonged to God,
and God turned out to be that guest.

*

The future takes a look at us
through its eyeglasses and facts.

The present scribbles letters to me
and lights signals for the signs it lacks:

imagination explores the past
and the future in the sea,

the past relays a baptismal
certificate in a song to me.

Through its eyeglasses and facts
the future takes a look at me.

*

The Lord multiplies His face:
my Image, please speak in my tongue!

From behind a cloud in the sky
God speaks in a Magyar song.

Yours is the land, so says the Lord,
but he leaves the rest untold:

All this is theirs, all that will pass,
the civil wars and the civil girls,
the holy shrouds and the holy mass,

God's friends and the future are they,
the heroes of the Coming Day;

all this belongs to the nation,
all this is the nation here,

the station garden and its guard,
the engine and the engineer
entering the railroad yard,

the nation's fate can reappear
in every son and daughter and its
6-3 football score over the Brits—

the newsboy hollers in the street,
the Daily Mail and Daily Rag;

regiments are changing guard,
the wind flutters a punctured flag;

all this is theirs and all are them,
the clouds and crowds of rebel men,

tough weeds of a dried-up fen.

I'll stay awake watching over them
as long as ten thousand years;
for me that's just a spell, from the first
rooster crow till the sun appears.

BALLAD OF JANTSI PEG LEG
(*Ballada Falábú Jancsiról*)

This is the ballad of Jantsi Peg Leg, nothing to do with me,
listen, you young mothers and you hip young man under the city tree,
and you too, innocent passersby, good folks, for these lines belong
to the toughest guy of the neighborhood—this is Jantsi Peg Leg's song.

        Jantsi Peg Leg's song.

A red spectre was haunting the parks
of our orphan, single-story land. Stealthily it smeared all with its cause.
Ill fate befell our poor toothless homeland:
it became the province of commander paws.
The province of crude commander paws.

Ay, ay,
a spectre was haunting this continent
called Europe and the whole world's hub,
and to quote the apt words of a famous poem,
all windows and doors got boarded up.

Boarded
        boarded
                securely boarded up,
all windows did, by prison guards.
Trilla-la, tralla-la,
And when they finally boarded up the Sun,
surely, surely, Jantsi Peg Leg
                        grabbed a gun!
And he armed his friends, every one.

Women were screaming in the food-store lines:
> Jantsi, don't give us a scare—for there was Peg
> Leg with a musket
the kind spectre-hunters bear,
> there was Peg Leg's wild smile.
Trilla, tralla, trallala,
> Jantsi, don't give us a scare.

There came the spectre, but it was no use,
the Jantsi's bunch locked it up
in an unbreakable last will
> or by some other ruse
they shut the sealed envelope on it
that's where they shut the spectre away.
  And sent it back to the sender.

> Perhaps the certified package was delivered to Red Square
> > or some other world
> and it was never returned
> it may never come back again
> > it may never come back again.

> But the spectre's teeth had wounded Jantsi in that fight.
> A nasty,
> > nasty,
> > > festering bite ...
> thus his death was a spectre-hunting accident.
> This ballad's from a grateful friend,

> and tells of Jantsi Peg Leg's tragic end.

Two Scenes from the drama Liberté '56

SCENE 85.
About Past Selection

PAVEL *and* SUSAN *in the girl's flat.*

PAVEL: Once I read it in the paper…

SUSAN: Which one?

PAVEL: The local newspaper.

SUSAN: What did it call itself?

PAVEL: The Barguzin Red Banner.

SUSAN: So one day the local paper…

PAVEL: … carried an announcement to the effect that from the first of the coming month everyone could choose his or her own past.

On the first day of the next month I went to the address given in the paper. The building was rather rundown. Some branch of law-enforcement authority operated in it.

I sat down in the waiting room on the mezzanine. I spoke to no one. I tried to catch the drift of the conversations around me, and I read an information sheet. It seemed to summarize everything one needed to know about past selection in a fairly   straightforward manner.

Anyone was free to choose any kind of past. There was even provision for those who were not happy with their new past; they could put in a request for a yet other one to replace the first choice for a substitute past.

As far as that is concerned, one cannot tell ahead of time whether one will like one's past or not; in other words, how one will feel being in that past after one gets into it. And another big question is whether the owner of a new past can be aware of possible disappointments in the same way he may be aware of the fact that he loathes the overcoat he picked out a few weeks earlier. That is, would it be possible to inform the owner of a new past that the old one fit him better after all?

SUSAN: You're fooling me!

PAVEL: Or to inform him of the possibility of an exchange for a totally different past. He'd have no idea that his past is not something he was born with and grew up with but that it's a past he picked out... Neither would he know where that office is where he acquired the past he regards as his and where he could exchange it for a new one in case he's unhappy with it.

SUSAN: Listen...

PAVEL: Unless he happens to come across that particular issue of the Barguzin Red Banner.

SUSAN: And among the various possible pasts...

PAVEL: Of course, every applicant had a choice of two kinds of past; one kind came with the awareness of it being a second past, and the other kind felt like the only possible past without any doubt as to its uniqueness and validity—as is the case normally with most people.

SUSAN: …and what kind did you…

PAVEL: For that reason, the new-past ownership manual included a manila envelope addressed to the new name if that was part of the new past, and in it there was detailed information about the past being the owner's own only to the extent that he himself had chosen it, but in the final analysis that past could not be regarded real.

SUSAN: But…

PAVEL: That's it! In the strict palpable sense of the word no past represents reality in the present, on the timescale we live in. So that was the sort of thing that was explained in that manila envelope—if there was such an envelope—on which under the owner's name there was a warning in bold print: TO BE OPENED ONLY IN DIRE EMERGENCY.

SUSAN: And none of this is true, is it?

PAVEL: What do you think?

*

SCENE 123.
The Bureau of Forgotten Things

The department of lost things was to the left at the top of the stairs and that of forgotten things to the right.

"I'd like to know all the things I've forgotten," I stepped in front of the old clerk manning the counter.

He barely raised his eyes from the crossword puzzle.

"We don't know who's forgotten all the things we store here..."

Then he corrected himself.

"... who are the people who have forgotten all these things."

He waved toward the lost items office.

"They don't know the rightful owners of all those umbrellas."

"But there I could at least see if there is anything belonging to me among those items."

"You can look here, too," the old man informed me. "And if you recognize something you used to know or something that happened to you, that's it. From then on you can recall those things, and we can cross them off on our list."

I had to think.

"And how many other people's memories do I have to look through before I can find my own?"

"It's a matter of chance," he answered immersing himself again in the puzzle.

"But what is the average time people spend here looking for their old desires, their loves, and their knowledge?"

"No time at all."

"How come?"

"When they find out you cannot request memories by name, belonging to one specific person, they give up."

"Aren't they curious about other people's memories?"

"I don't know."

"About, for example, how they themselves might crop up among other people's memories."

"Among other people's forgotten memories?" asked the clerk. And then he went on: "Yes, I expect it may occur to some of our clientele. But it's not a big crowd. Our bureau is not well-known in the general population."

I took a cursory look through the archives. But I didn't get beyond the closest shelves. This is not something I've forgotten; no, this is not mine; this is not either. My God, I sighed, where could all those things be that I've forgotten.

Finally the clerk looked up from the crossword puzzle.

"Tell me, could you help me by any chance? A festive and plentiful social meal. Seven letters."

"Seven letters? Banquet." I answered.

"Banquet … Yes, of course," he glanced up at me. "I used to know that. I knew it for sure at one time. But I'd forgotten."

BIOGRAPHICAL NOTES

GÉZA SZŐCS

poet, writer, journalist and politician, was born in Marosvásárhely, Târgu Mureş (Erdély, Transylvania, part of Romania since 1920), in 1953 into the Hungarian community where he was raised.

Géza Szőcs in 1983

He published his first volume of poetry in 1975 (Kriterion Publishing House, Bucharest) while still a student majoring in Hungarian and Russian at the Babeş–Bolyai University in Kolozsvár, Cluj-Napoca, Romania. After graduation in 1978 he worked for a newspaper until 1979 when he studied at the University of Vienna on a Herder Scholarship for a year. Back in Romania his journalistic and literary career was hampered by harassment from the Securitate, the grim secret police, for his underground activities on behalf of his ethnic minority as well as the human rights of the whole Romanian society. Finally in 1986 he was forced into exile in Switzerland until the regime change. Since then he supplemented his writing career with various political and editorial positions in Hungary.

The poet would have been simply jailed instead of exiled had it not been for the intervention of American writers and politicians who asked the Romanian government and party leaders to refrain from the persecution of dissenters. Among the politicians who spoke up on this issue were Rep. Tom Lantos from California, Rep. Bernard J. Dwyer of New Jersey and Sen. Chris Dodd of Connecticut; among the writers were Susan Sontag and William Least Heat Moon, a Native American writer to whom Szőcs expressed his gratitude in a poem that was subsequently published in numerous translations and is included in this book. He also reached out to Gloria Steinem in an open letter that exposed the cruel way Romanian women were subjected to obligatory gynaecological control every two months (pregnancy tests) in order to prevent their attempts at abortion. Géza Szőcs was the only one to raise his voice against this barbaric practice by the government.

In addition, through his translations he acquainted the Hungarian reading public with Emily Dickinson, Robinson Jeffers, Charles Bernstein, and Charles Olson. His own poetry was translated by such prominent writers as George Szirtes and appeared in a number of publications such as *Sulfur Magazine, Absinthe Poetry Review*, etc. He valued his contact with Robert Creeley and Clayton Eshleman.

Thus it is hard to understand why in spite of all these personal and intellectual connections he is not better known in the United States while his volumes of poetry have been published in German, Italian, Polish, Romanian, Russian, Swedish, Croatian, Chinese and Spanish translation and his poetry has been praised by such world figures as Mikhail Gorbachev, Uri Geller, György Kurtág, Krzysztof Penderecki and Andrzej Wajda. Among other awards he was the recipient of the much-valued Italian Giacomo Leopardi Prize. This slender volume is his much-delayed debut in the Anglophone literary world.

The poet's professional political life started after leaving his country when he played an important role in the events leading up to the fall of communism in both Hungary and Romania. He was a contributing editor to Radio Free Europe (an institution supported by US Congress); he also founded and headed up its office in Budapest. The regime change propelled him into leading political positions in both countries.

Presently he is the president of the Hungarian Centre of International PEN. As such he is the head curator of the Janus Pannonius Prize, one of the world's most coveted poetry prizes. Other important members of the curatorial committee are Marjorie Perloff, literary critic, Enikő Bollobás, literary scholar, Tomaso Kemeny, poet and translator and Dorin Tudoran, a prominent Romanian poet now living in Washington, D.C.

Endre Wellmann Farkas

PAUL SOHAR

came to the U.S. from Hungary as a student refugee where he got a BA degree in philosophy and a day job in chemistry while he con-

Paul Sohar

tinued writing and publishing in every genre, including thirteen volumes of translations such as *Dancing Embers*, his first Sándor Kányádi translations from the Hungarian (Twisted Spoon Press, 2002). His own poetry: *Homing Poems* (Iniquity Press, 2006) and *The Wayward Orchard*, a Wordrunner Press Prize winner (2011). Other awards: first prize in the 2012 Lincoln Poets Society contest and a second prize from Rhode Island Writers Circle prose contest (2014). Latest translation volumes: *Silver Pirouettes* (poems by George Faludy, TheWriteDeal 2012) and *In Contemporary Tense* (more Kányádi poems, Iniquity Press, 2013) in addition to a bilingual (English/ Spanish) Sándor Kányádi volume (*Under the Southern Cross*, Ragged Sky Press, 2015). Prose works: *True Tales of a Fictitious Spy* published by SynergeBooks in 2006 and four one-act plays published by One Act Depot in Saskatchewan, Canada, 2013 and 2014. Magazine credits include *Agni, Gargoyle, Kenyon Review, Rattle, Poetry Salzburg Review, Seneca Review, etc.* His translation work has been recognized by prizes such as the Irodalmi Jelen Translation Prize (2014), Tóth Árpád Translation Prize and the Janus Pannonius Lifetime Achievement Award (both in 2016, Budapest, Hungary).

ADDENDA

Politics looms high behind many of Szőcs's poems and dominates some of them; moreover, the poet personally engaged in underground political activities, which mostly involved trying to enlighten his fellow citizens and the outside world about things the communist propaganda tried to hide before the regime change in 1989. The letter below illustrates not only the kind of information he wanted to pass on to influential people in the West, but also the difficulty of the project: this open letter—whether it ever reached its intended recipient or not—may have contributed to the amelioration of the brutal measures it protested, but eventually it also resulted in the expulsion of its writer from Romania. Writings such as this made up the samizdat literature of the political underground. This translation preserved much of the idiosyncratic punctuation and the redundancies as evidence of the writer's emotional state and the urgency of the matter on hand.

Géza Szőcs:
Letter to Ms. Gloria Steinem

The spiritual bubonic plague now spreading all over Romania—look, another embarrassing boil!—has enriched the manual of social diseases with a new chapter. The state-power structure that had already assumed the right to oversee not only all social functions and activities, but also the right to monitor totally the personal lives of individuals—but why bother talking about legal rights?—in other words, the authority of the state that claims to be the heir to a two-thousand-year-old culture, has come up with a novel form of law enforcement. In any case, the idea is unprecedented in history; at best, it may look somewhat familiar from the projections of dystopian societies into the future or particularly depressing sci-fi novels. What I am talking about is a new health regulation promulgated by the Romanian state bureaucracy that orders all women between the ages of 15 and 45 to report every two months for an obligatory gynaecological examination. Any woman whose condition is found suspicious will be kept under close observation by the authorities in order to prevent her from denying the state a new citizen. What do you call this if not phallocracy armed with the political power of the state?

In addition, I have to remind you that in Romania all forms of contraception—other than abstinence—are strictly forbidden by law. Abstinence is still legally allowed. (On the other hand, abstinence is highly taxed: childless persons above the age of 25 have to pay an enormously high childlessness tax.) In our country gynecologists have no right to prescribe birth-control pills for their patients. Romanian customs officers and border guards, usually very interested in forbidden printed material, are even more eager to keep an eye out for condoms, pills, and IUDs possibly smuggled in by visitors from abroad. Any doctor performing abortion and any patient undergoing it risk a prison sentence of many years.

Thus, in our country there is no civilized way of avoiding pregnancy. Women, whether aged 16 or 44, who have no right to decide if they want to carry the child from an unwanted pregnancy—this is decided for them by others—now face the ordeal of being laid on their back, stripped and searched in their private parts by the paws of the state. (Incidentally, a hygienic detail may be added to the procedure that—like most things in Romania— the implementation of the law was not well organized, and the shortage of hygienic supplies in many clinics forces the doctors to examine 10 or 15 women using the same latex gloves.)

But Madam, if you were to make an official inquiry into this matter, the answer you will get is easy for me to predict. First of all, without batting an eye, they will deny the whole thing. But if let us say you were to present irrefutable evidence, the answer will be simple: the compulsory test has nothing to do with pregnancy! It is simply a normal, routine health measure. What it proves is nothing but the unlimited humanitarian care our Party and State lavishes on us.

A statement like that is not easy to refute; however, you Madam can decide for yourself. If fighter pilots are required to take a medical exam only once a year, how come all otherwise healthy women must undergo a gynaecological exam every 60 days? (The 45-year age limit should raise a red flag; it is usually at that age the health problems begin to crop up. How curious the coincidence: Romanian women under the age of 45 are required by law to let pregnancy take its course, but those between the ages of 45 and 85 are free to terminate it. The correlation is worth noting: abortion under the age of 45 is banned by law, and it is women in this age bracket who are required to report for the frequent medical exams. And that attention is paid only to women; the state shows no such concern about the health of men, even if they work in lead mines or glass-blowing shops.)

Seeing women—who may be themselves, their mothers, their wives, their fiancées, their sisters, their daughters—so disenfranchised, so humiliated, so dispossessed of human dignity, Romanians should be going around with their ears flaming red from shame, instead of putting up with the situation without uttering a word of protest.

Being a man is not much easier in Romania. A Romanian citizen is not allowed to purchase land; he is punished with a jail sentence if he slaughters his own cow, and has to pay a heavy fine if he puts up a stranger even for one night in his own house, or if he makes more than three international calls a month from his own phone. A citizen may have no more than a few grams of gold and no foreign currency of any kind; that entails years of imprisonment. (A Romanian tourist can travel to the West—and lately even to the other countries of the socialist bloc—only if someone in the country of his destination guarantees that his expenses will be covered. A citizen of our country—attention!: it's forbidden to take Romanian currency out of the country!—must leave the territory of Romania without a penny in his pocket. Of course, travel abroad is also regulated by law: only once every two years, and only if he can get a passport, which he can hardly call his own; it is held by the police, not by him.) Moreover, all valuable books and art objects in private possession are under the guardianship of the National Art Preservation Commission. If someone builds a house with a lifetime of effort, he must be prepared to see it demolished without notice in return for a nominal restitution. (Provided it is not confiscated first on the advice of the National Estate Control Commission.) Officially, there is no unemployment in Romania, but every year thousands lose their jobs because of reorganization, and they have to find new employment on their own. What is mandated by law in Switzerland—such as keeping food reserves always on hand—is considered a crime in Romania.

The list is endless, I could go on forever, but there's no need for that: it is clear from the foregoing that the concept of home has become just as illusory as the situation concerning private property. BUT UP UNTIL NOW EVEN IF ROMANIAN CITIZENS KNEW THEY COULD NOT REGARD THEIR JOBS, THEIR LAND, THEIR FARM ANIMALS, THEIR HOMES, THEIR TELEPHONES, THEIR PASSPORTS, THEIR PAINTINGS, THEIR WORK CAPACITY, THEIR LIVES (THAT TOO BELONGS TO THE HOMELAND) AS THEIR OWN: BUT AT LEAST THEY COULD CONSIDER THEIR BODIES MORE

OR LESS THEIR OWN. Up until now we thought that on June 11, 1948 only large landholdings and industrial plants were nationalized—and now, 37 years later it turns out that women's wombs too are nationalized. In general, the state considers women as a separate race, tools for producing population, as no more than animals kept for breeding.

How about the fetus? Already at fetus age the fetus will get used to being frisked and searched and later on in life he will take it for granted as the natural course of events. And all these things are happening in the very Romania, which is considered by many from the West as one of the freest communist countries, even though similar conditions cannot be found anywhere else in Europe or in even worse places in the world.

Considering all the above, Madam, you should not be surprised that Romanian women are not too happy to bring children into this world—and I have not even started talking about food supply that is available to the population, which is totally inadequate when it comes to basic needs, such as milk, powdered milk, butter or meat. Going further: in some of the neighboring communist countries like Hungary, state-supported maternity leave lasts several years—in Romania it's only three months. But Madam, I don't want to overburden you. The gist is this: the above-described mood of the people will not be improved by any kind of demagoguery about the beauty of raising children and—as the local media constantly asserts—how no other country in history has ever done more for children than the Romanian state of today. If that were true, the state would not have to hunt for future subjects in women's wombs.

Under these conditions, would-be mothers—instead of giving birth in a country like this—will rather take a chance and trust their bodies to black-market health providers, village midwives, quacks, and witches who make angels out of the fetuses with their primitive, handmade instruments. This practice results in numberless tragedies as the unintended consequences of a narrow-minded and violently enforced idea: a great number of young girls lose their lives, those who later would have given birth to one or two or perhaps more children if they had not sacrificed themselves—or been sacrificed—on the altar of great power aspirations. This way Romania is not going to catch up with China or India as measured in terms of population—as it was imagined in Bucharest—but instead it will diminish its biological potential.

After all this, it should be especially understandable why women are not eager to give birth, and even more especially understandable with regard to women who belong to ethnic groups—other than Romanian. Personally, I don't agree with them, but the fact is that these women, mostly Hungarian and German, find in this (too) a way to protest against the anti-minority policy of assimilation that now defines Romania's internal political life. In other words: they don't want to give birth to children who will be assimilated by the state, not only politically but also in their language, no matter what means the state might deem necessary to deploy. According to statistics, the state is scoring a success so far.

Romania has an over two-million-strong Hungarian ethnic group. I too belong to it. On that basis, some people might wonder what right does a Hungarian man have to protest in the name of Romanian women? Well, for one thing, naturally, I am not protesting in the name of women but in the interest of women. And I do so in the name of something they used to call a moral society.

Another thing: the ethnic minorities are required to submit to the same fate forced upon the national majority by their own political leadership.—If that's the way it has to be, if in fact the power of the state does not distinguish between Romanians and members of national minorities in this respect, then—paraphrasing a well-known Romanian saying, we too can say: IF YOU PEOPLE WANT US, WE TOO WANT YOU. If indeed we must accept the fate of the majority—if in this manner they force us to join the majority—then in this particular respect I consider myself as belonging to the majority. In that case, I assume to have gained the right from the majority to declare in the name of the majority: I PROTEST. I protest against the slap on the face delivered to women, I protest against a practice that diminishes their dignity, human dignity in general, and the dignity of the Romanian nation, too—because in fact not only women are treated as breeding animals but the whole country is becoming an animal farm. (Yes, I say animal farm, but the practice that's being implemented here goes well beyond Orwell's power of imagination.) I protest, because I find it shameful and despicable what's happening here, especially the fact that no one is willing to raise his voice against this situation.

For the sake of the truth, I feel compelled to say: for the time being, not only women belonging to the party aristocracy are exempt from the law, but also some members of the intelligentsia. Our doctors started their work relying on the health network of the villages and the factory workers. This allows them to test the largest number of women with a minimum of bother (in factory health clinics, during working hours, etc.). The implementation of the practice on the more dispersed and possibly more resistant college-educated class is now in preparation.

Finally this: the only ally Romanian women can count on in this matter is nothing but the usual shortcomings typical of our country: poor organization, laziness, poor work ethics, sloppiness, and the usual fatigue and boredom the gigantic projects and unending campaigns elicit from the overburdened population. That's the only hope women can entertain concerning this practice, that slowly, almost unnoticeably, it will be abandoned. It's a practice that would invalidate the place of any country among cultured nations.

Madam, in the hope that I was able to enlighten you concerning an issue that might be of interest to you—as the world-renowned and unrelenting spokesperson on behalf of women's equality, and with the request that you share your thoughts with me if indeed this issue has attracted your attention—I remain your sincerest fan,

Géza Szőcs
Kolozsvár (Cluj), Oct. 2, 1985

A Note on Transylvanian History

The earliest records show Transylvania belonging to Dacia, a Roman province at the very frontiers of the Empire. Then for a thousand years Transylvania was the home of Hungarians in coexistence with Romanians and other ethnic communities.

In the Trianon treaty after WW I Romania obtained the eastern part of historical Hungary, including Transylvania, from a disintegrating Austro-Hungarian Empire. Thus the Hungarian population in that region sank into minority status which was especially oppressive under the Communist dictator Ceausescu who tried to curry favor with his subjects by blaming all ills on minorities, most of all ethnic Hungarians—the favorite and sure-fire weapon of all totalitarian systems. But things are slow to change even now; democracy is new to the region and support for minority rights is not compatible with the prevailing attitude that regards other ethnic groups as enemies. For example, an eight-hundred-year-old German community was completely driven out of the country in the decades before the fall of communism in 1989. Since then the officially sanctioned persecution by the police state has been replaced by informal, random acts of hate. But at least, it did not turn into another Bosnia. There's still hope for peaceful coexistence, but it helps to let the world know that there is a thriving, thousand-year-old Hungarian community in Transylvania.

Most poems in this book date from the time of the Ceausescu dictatorship.

Paul Sohar

CPSIA information can be obtained
at www.ICGtesting.com
Printed in the USA
FFOW05n2055040617

9 789737 842312